THE BEATLES

FOR OCARINA

2	All My Loving	17	In My Life
3	And I Love Her	18	Lady Madonna
4	Blackbird	20	Let It Be
5	Can't Buy Me Love	19	The Long and Winding Road
6	Come Together	22	Lucy in the Sky with Diamonds
7	Eight Days a Week	23	Michelle
8	Eleanor Rigby	24	Norwegian Wood (This Bird Has Flown)
9	The Fool on the Hill	25	Nowhere Man
10	A Hard Day's Night	26	Ob-La-Di, Ob-La-Da
11	Here Comes the Sun	27	Penny Lane
12	Here, There and Everywhere	28	Something
13	Hey Jude	29	We Can Work It Out
14	I Saw Her Standing There	30	With a Little Help from My Friends
15	I Want to Hold Your Hand	31	Yellow Submarine
16	I Will	32	Yesterday

The ocarina on the front cover is available at www.halleonard.com, item HL00369336.

ISBN 978-1-70513-826-7

Visit Hal Leonard Online at
www.halleonard.com

Contact us:
Hal Leonard
7777 West Bluemound Road
Milwaukee, WI 53213
Email: info@halleonard.com

In Europe, contact:
Hal Leonard Europe Limited
42 Wigmore Street
Marylebone, London, W1U 2RN
Email: info@halleonardeurope.com

In Australia, contact:
Hal Leonard Australia Pty. Ltd.
4 Lentara Court
Cheltenham, Victoria, 3192 Australia
Email: info@halleonard.com.au

ALL MY LOVING

from A HARD DAY'S NIGHT

OCARINA

Words and Music by JOHN LENNON
and PAUL McCARTNEY

AND I LOVE HER

OCARINA

Words and Music by JOHN LENNON
and PAUL McCARTNEY

BLACKBIRD

OCARINA

Words and Music by JOHN LENNON
and PAUL McCARTNEY

Slowly and smoothly

CAN'T BUY ME LOVE

OCARINA

Words and Music by JOHN LENNON
and PAUL McCARTNEY

COME TOGETHER

OCARINA

Words and Music by JOHN LENNON
and PAUL McCARTNEY

EIGHT DAYS A WEEK

OCARINA

Words and Music by JOHN LENNON
and PAUL McCARTNEY

ELEANOR RIGBY

OCARINA

Words and Music by JOHN LENNON
and PAUL McCARTNEY

Moderately

THE FOOL ON THE HILL

OCARINA

Words and Music by JOHN LENNON
and PAUL McCARTNEY

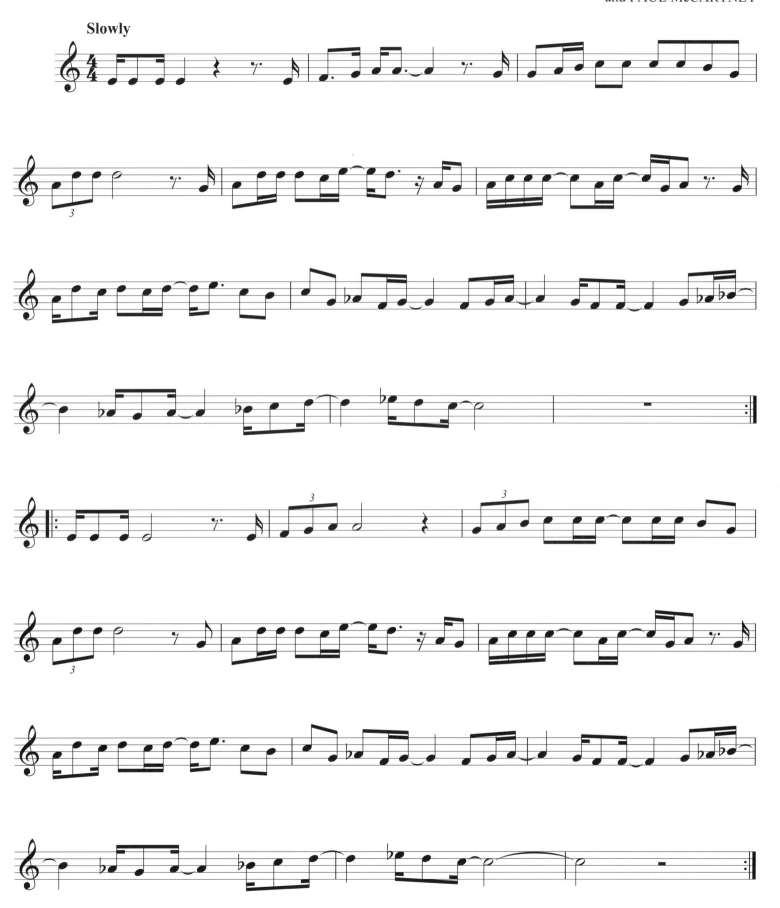

A HARD DAY'S NIGHT

OCARINA

Words and Music by JOHN LENNON
and PAUL McCARTNEY

HERE COMES THE SUN

OCARINA

Words and Music by
GEORGE HARRISON

HERE, THERE AND EVERYWHERE

OCARINA

Words and Music by JOHN LENNON
and PAUL McCARTNEY

HEY JUDE

OCARINA

Words and Music by JOHN LENNON
and PAUL McCARTNEY

I SAW HER STANDING THERE

OCARINA

Words and Music by JOHN LENNON
and PAUL McCARTNEY

I WANT TO HOLD YOUR HAND

OCARINA

Words and Music by JOHN LENNON
and PAUL McCARTNEY

Moderately, with a beat

I WILL

OCARINA

Words and Music by JOHN LENNON
and PAUL McCARTNEY

IN MY LIFE

OCARINA

Words and Music by JOHN LENNON
and PAUL McCARTNEY

LADY MADONNA

OCARINA

Words and Music by JOHN LENNON
and PAUL McCARTNEY

Brightly

THE LONG AND WINDING ROAD

OCARINA

Words and Music by JOHN LENNON
and PAUL McCARTNEY

LET IT BE

OCARINA

Words and Music by JOHN LENNON
and PAUL McCARTNEY

LUCY IN THE SKY WITH DIAMONDS

OCARINA

Words and Music by JOHN LENNON
and PAUL McCARTNEY

MICHELLE

OCARINA

Words and Music by JOHN LENNON
and PAUL McCARTNEY

NORWEGIAN WOOD
(This Bird Has Flown)

OCARINA

Words and Music by JOHN LENNON
and PAUL McCARTNEY

NOWHERE MAN

OCARINA

Words and Music by JOHN LENNON
and PAUL McCARTNEY

Moderately bright

To Coda

D.C. al Coda   **CODA**

OB-LA-DI, OB-LA-DA

OCARINA

Words and Music by JOHN LENNON
and PAUL McCARTNEY

PENNY LANE

OCARINA

Words and Music by JOHN LENNON
and PAUL McCARTNEY

SOMETHING

OCARINA

Words and Music by
GEORGE HARRISON

WE CAN WORK IT OUT

OCARINA

Words and Music by JOHN LENNON
and PAUL McCARTNEY

WITH A LITTLE HELP FROM MY FRIENDS

OCARINA

Words and Music by JOHN LENNON
and PAUL McCARTNEY

YELLOW SUBMARINE

OCARINA

Words and Music by JOHN LENNON
and PAUL McCARTNEY

YESTERDAY

OCARINA

Words and Music by JOHN LENNON
and PAUL McCARTNEY

Moderately, with expression